The Wing Wing Brothers

MATH SPECTACULAR!

WILLY

WILMER

WALTER

WOODY

WENDELL

BY ETHAN LONG

Holiday House / New York

Ladies and gentlemen, children of all ages! We welcome you to the most amazing, most astounding show on Earth!
Introducing . . .

Wendell has one plate. Wilmer has one plate.

= is an equal sign.
It shows two amounts
having the same value.

1 = 1

Willy sends two more plates.

> means greater than. It shows one value is larger than another.

3 > 1

Wendell has three plates. Wilmer has one plate.

Woody tosses four more plates.

3 < 5

Now Wendell only has three plates. Wilmer has five plates.

< means less than. It shows one value is smaller than another.

Wendell will not wait.

8 > 5

Wendell now has eight plates. Willy still has five plates.

Wendell gets two more plates. Wilmer gets five more plates

Now Wendell and Wilmer have the same number.

Now Wendell and Wilmer have the same number again.

ACT 2
Addition and Subtraction

Willy has one pie.

+ means plus.

Wilmer tosses another pie to Willy.

1 + 1 = 2

Presto! Another pie appears.

2 + 1 = 3

Plop! One pie drops.

$$3 + 1 = 4$$

Wow! Willy has four pies.

Prepare for one more pie.

 Willy has five pies.

Pow! Pow! Pow! Pow!

5 - 4 = 1 Willy has one pie left.

Bye, bye, pie.

1 - 1 = 0 Now all the pies are gone.

Woody wheels out a box.

Woody is one bird.

Walter, Willy, Wendell, and Wilmer come out of the box.

1 + 4 = 5 Now there are five brothers.

Wilmer and Willy are going back into the box.

Walter, Woody, and Wendell are three brothers.

Wow! **5 – 2 = 3** Only three brothers are left.

Wheee! Wilmer is back. **3 + 1 = 4** Now there are four brothers.

What? Woody is gone. **4 − 1 = 3** Now there are three brothers.

Wait!

Walter is not gone. 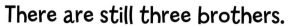 There are still three brothers.

Whoa! Where are Walter, Wendell, and Wilmer?

3 - 3 = 0   Now there are zero brothers.

Pee-yew!

$$0 + 5 = 5$$

The Common Core State Standards

This book meets the Common Core State Standards for kindergarten mathematics in Counting and Cardinality: identify whether the number of objects in one group is greater than, less than, or equal to the number of objects in another group (K.CC.6) and compare two numbers between 1 and 10 presented as written numerals (K.CC.7). It also meets the standards for kindergarten mathematics in Operations and Algebraic Thinking: understand addition as putting together and adding to, and understand subtraction as taking apart and taking from (K.OA.1-5).

The publisher would like to thank Grace Wilkie for reviewing this book for accuracy. Grace is the past president of the Association of Mathematics Teachers of New York State and New York State Mathematics Honor Society as well as an expert on Common Core Standards, National Council of Teachers of Mathematics Standards, and New York State Mathematics Standards.

To Mrs. Kennedy,
Media Specialist
Extraordinaire

Printed and Bound in March 2012 at Tien Wah Press,
Johor Bahru, Johor, Malaysia.
The text typeface is Billy.
The artwork was created with black Prismacolor pencils
on bristol board and colored digitally on a Mac.
www.holidayhouse.com
First Edition
1 3 5 7 9 10 8 6 4 2

Library of Congress Cataloging-in-Publication Data
Long, Ethan.
The Wing Wing brothers math spectacular! / Ethan Long. — 1st ed.
p. cm.
ISBN 978-0-8234-2320-0 (hardcover)
1. Numeration—Study and teaching (Primary) 2. Numbers, Natural—
Study and teaching (Primary) I. Title.
QA141.L74 2012
372.7—dc23
2011018256